Amy, I love you! You come from a position becau
qualified that you expect that people are as highly qualified as you. Others
can learn from you about how to find the right professional. So, they are
not going to get crappy advice. We see bad advice all the time and you must
clean it up. She helps people, and owners build their businesses, and grow
their businesses in ways that, well, frankly you may never have thought
about. You are so detail oriented with what you do.

Ken Krell, Amazing Digital Events

Amy Herrick is a "ROCKSTAR" ! I absolutely loved having her as a guest
on my podcast as well as on my live stream. She has so much value to give
that having one conversation is not enough. I highly recommend Amy as a
guest speaker, you will not be disappointed, but you will be amazed at her
wealth of knowledge. Amy Rose is just amazing. She is great at what she
does. She will help you build your business correctly with the right
foundations.

Laquita Monley, La Quita's ToolBox Podcast

I love what you are doing. You have so much knowledge. I love finding
people who have just a little bit of a different perspective on things because
it makes you think. I've always kind of been questioning if the crowd's
doing it, is it right? I do not know. Is it a group thing? You've given me a
ton of value.

Chris Gunkle , Unrivaled Experts

Whatever you got that involves detailed numbers, you will not find, in my
estimate, a more thorough, careful, helpful hand. You cannot do better.

Artie Vipperla, Psychic Grandmaster, Energy Healer & Spiritual Guide

Amy's book was a fun read. As a Personal Historian, I loved the information about ways to use your smartphone more efficiently. We even included that section in a new book about interviewing elderly relatives for a family history. Hurrah for Smart Cookies, who make this a better world.

Judy Helm Wright—Author/Historian/IntuitiveWiseWoman

Money with Amy Series

The Profitable Entrepreneur:

16 Ways to Retrain Entrepreneurs Using Mindset, Time Management, Leveraging Your Resources and Enjoying More Business Travel Inexpensively

Free Audio Version Included

Amy Rose Herrick, ChFC
Profit-Building Specialist
International Best-Selling Author
Published by Amy Rose Herrick

Herrick, Amy Rose

The Profitable Entrepreneur: 16 Ways to Retrain Entrepreneurs Using Mindset, Time Management, Leveraging Your Resources and Enjoying More Business Travel Inexpensively

First edition PDF version

Christiansted, US Virgin Islands: Amy Rose Herrick, 2024

xviii, 98, 9 inches

Entrepreneur | Self-employment | | Independent Contractor | Sole Proprietor | Single Member LLC | Finances | Mindset | Business Travel | Mailing list valuations | Cyber Security | Voice to text | Bartering |

978-1-960427-25-0
LCCN 2023951264
658.421

Amy Rose Herrick's books may be purchased in bulk for premiums, groups, educational, business or sales promotional use. For information, please write to: Amy@AmyRoseHerrick.com.

Disclaimer: The information and/or documents contained in this book do not constitute legal or financial advice and should never be used without first consulting with other professionals to determine what may be best for your individual needs. The publisher and the author do not make any guarantee or other promise as to any results that may be obtained from using the content of this book. The publisher and the author make no guarantees concerning the level of success you may experience by following the advice and strategies contained in this book, and you accept the risk that results will differ

DEDICATION

This book is dedicated to all the visionary entrepreneurs and business owners who dare to dream, take risks, and strive for greatness.

Your determination and relentless pursuit of success inspire us all.

This book is dedicated to you—the innovators, the creators, and the trailblazers—whose passion and resilience fuel the engine of progress.

May these pages serve as a guiding light on your entrepreneurial journey, empowering you to overcome challenges, embrace opportunities, and achieve your boldest aspirations.

Your dedication to making a difference in the world is a testament to the true spirit of entrepreneurship.

Thank you for being the driving force behind positive change, and for inspiring others to fearlessly pursue their dreams.

Content

Introduction:

Unleash Your Entrepreneurial Success!

Welcome, fellow solo-preneurs and entrepreneurs! I am thrilled to have you embark on this transformative journey with me. In this book, we will explore the essential tools and strategies to elevate your business game and achieve unprecedented success.

Section One is all about adjusting your entrepreneur mindset, and we kick things off in Chapter 1 with a revelation that will change the way you approach business forever. Get ready to master the multiplying power of "10." This secret gem will show you how to turn slight changes into monumental profits over time, setting you on the path to financial abundance.

Chapter 2 takes a whimsical turn as we delve into the quirky side of ASAP. Urgency meets cartoon wisdom in a lesson that will redefine how you communicate with others and manage expectations. Discover the true essence of ASAP and its impact on your business dynamics.

Do you struggle to be quote-worthy? Chapter 3 will unveil the hidden talent within you. Learn how to craft captivating and insightful quotes in under a minute. By the end of this chapter, you will be armed with words that inspire and resonate with your audience, establishing you as a thought leader in your field.

Section Two is a revelation, exposing the missed opportunities in your business. Chapter 4 draws parallels between business and the classic board game Monopoly, revealing timeless lessons that can shape your success. From negotiating like a pro to embracing competition, you will uncover essential strategies to thrive in the entrepreneurial world.

Numbers and financial statements can seem intimidating but fear not! In Chapter 5, we simplify financial statements to make them as easy to understand as your 5-year-old self's piggy bank. You will gain the confidence to analyze your financial data and make informed decisions that steer your business towards prosperity.

Chapter 6 introduces an invaluable skill - valuing your mailing list. Every email address holds potential profits, and we will show you five methods to determine the true worth of each contact. Empower your online business and leverage the power of your mailing list for growth and success.

The digital age brings both opportunities and risks. Chapter 7 emphasizes the importance of cybersecurity for every business. Learn about creating a WISP (Written Information Security Program) to safeguard your business against cyber threats, ensuring the safety of your valuable data and customer trust.

Section Three dives into the critical relationship between your time and money. In Chapter 8, we guide you through a quick and painless process of calculating your net worth. Understanding your financial standing gives you a solid foundation for better decision-making and future financial growth.

In Chapter 9, we dispel the myth that dictations are obsolete. Explore the wonders of modern speech-to-text technology and how it can revolutionize your productivity and efficiency in running your business and the many free or almost free resources to do so!

Chapter 10 is all about maximizing profits through efficient equipment usage. Discover the transformative power of extra monitors, laptops, and printers/scanners, as we reveal the potential, they hold to boost your productivity and bottom line.

Section Four introduces innovative financing strategies for your business. In Chapter 11, we explore the world of Self-Directed Retirement Accounts, unlocking a new realm of possibilities for business and property acquisition. Get ready to tap into an unconventional and powerful funding source.

Chapter 12 is all about turning small investments into significant returns. We will show you how to earn impressive percentages on modest amounts, making your money work harder for you.

Do not waste time on unprofitable endeavors. Chapter 13 urges you to stop bartering unproductive items and focus on optimizing your resources for better results with a method to calculate the answer too!

Finally, Section Five will let you in on the secrets to travel like a pro. Chapter 14 reveals the magic of using SkyScanner for budget-friendly international travel, enabling you to explore the world without breaking the bank.

Chapter 15 unveils the top money-saving tips for booking airline tickets with Google Flights, empowering you to find the best deals for your air travel needs if you prefer this travel platform.

In the last chapter, Chapter 16, we will share valuable insights on boosting productivity during business trips by leveraging vacation rentals and short-term apartments. Travel smart and make the most of your business journeys.

Are you ready to transform your entrepreneurial journey and soar to new heights of success? Let us begin this adventure together and unlock the secrets to a thriving and fulfilling business life. Here is the roadmap to unleashing your entrepreneurial success!

To access your free audio version, please use this link:

https://www.moneywithamyaudiobo oks.com/the-profitable-entrepreneur-16-ways-to-retrain-entrepreneurs

Section One- Adjusting Your Entrepreneur Mindset

Chapter 1:

Mastering the multiplying power of "10"

MONEY WITH AMY SERIES

THE PROFITABLE ENTREPRENEUR:
16 Ways to Retrain Entrepreneurs
Using Mindset, Time Management,
Leveraging Your Resources and
Enjoying More Business Travel Inexpensively

How would you like to learn a new skill to start using right now as you begin making changes to increase your profitability?

Do you know about the secret power of "10"?

I bet you are thinking "What is that all about? I have never heard anyone talking about the secret power of "10". "

What is the secret power of "10" most business owners do not know?

The secret power of "10" is when you take the annual savings you create by a change in business behavior or operations times "10" years.

This is the amount you can add to your profits over time if you plan to keep the business long term.

If you plan to sell the business in a few years, it could be three or five years, then use that number instead of "10" for your expected selling timeline.

This is a mental game changing revelation when you start to see how every change big and small can leap your profits into levels you never dreamed were possible before you learned the secret power of "10".

You can experience profit increases now. But whenever a change is measurable, you can visualize the long-term cumulative cash flow effect on your profitability.

How life changing will it be for you and your loved ones to harness the secret power of "10"?

Will you take more time off during the week and longer leisure vacations?

Will you buy a dream home?

Will you expand your business?

Will you be able to pay for college tuitions, weddings, cars, and other things you struggle to even think about now?

What would you do if finances were no longer holding you back from touching your dreams?

To help you start seeing a more profitable future, I will be using the power of "10" in my examples. These examples will help you get comfortable using the power of "10" in all your future financial decisions.

Now it is time to start making you more profitable!

On the next page is your blueprint for calculating the potential economic impact to your bottom line when changes are considered.

Yu will see how multiplying a change times ten years completely changes your perspective of any change you decide to implement.

Profitability from Change Worksheet

By the day $ _____ x _____ days in the week change will occur
x _____ weeks = $_____Annual savings

By the week $ _____ x _____ number of weeks the change will occur =
                                   $_____Annual savings

By the month $ _____ x _____ months change will occur =
                                   $_____Annual savings

Total annual potential increase in profits $_____
Less cost to implement, if any   -_____
Net potential increase in profits $_____

Net potential increase in profits X 5 years $_____

Net potential increase in profits X 10 years $_____

Is it worth our time to implement this change?

Yes or No (Circle one)

What did we change? _____

Why did we change it? _____

Who is responsible for implementing changes? _____

_____

Target dates of status reports if needed: _____

_____

Target date change will be fully integrated. _____

Chapter 2:

ASAP Requires a Modern Translation: Anxious? Seek Another Person!

MONEY WITH AMY SERIES

THE PROFITABLE ENTREPRENEUR:
16 Ways to Retrain Entrepreneurs
Using Mindset, Time Management,
Leveraging Your Resources and
Enjoying More Business Travel Inexpensively

What does it truly mean when we hear others casually throw around the phrase "I'll take care of that ASAP"? I am an entrepreneur, and I am not sure everyone else understands this phrase like I interpret it.

You see, when most of us employ the term ASAP in any setting, we tend to think in terms of what ASAP means to us personally, not to the person on the other side of the conversation.

You may be thinking you heard the shortened version of "As Soon As Possible." I am no longer certain that is indeed the right translation.

The next time you find yourself getting worked up and upset because someone is not addressing your concern ASAP, per your ASAP definition standards, breath, perhaps it is time to reflect on a few of the many different possible meanings of ASAP.

Just for clarity, why not ask the next person who tells you they will do what you asked "ASAP," to define their version of ASAP that is cleverly hidden from public view?

Here are a few unique versions of ASAP to ponder to start out on the lighter side if "As Soon As Possible" is not the definition of the day you expected.

Anxious? Seek Another Person!

After September, April Possibly.

As Slow As Penguins…

Avoiding Serious Action, Pal!

Absolutely Stagnant, Achievements Pending.

Alright, Someday, Absolutely, Promise!

After Several Attempts, Perhaps…

Absolutely Stalling And Procrastinating.

At Snail's Ambling Pace.

Amazingly Slow, Avoiding Progress.

Always Skipping Actual Priorities!

Annoyingly Slow And Painful

Avoiding Serious Assignments. Postponed!

Absentmindedly, Saying Anything Promising...

After Several Aimless Promises...

Ahem, Sabotaging Any Productivity.

Absurdly Slow. Ahh...Postponement!
Amusing, Silly, Answer Provided

Absolute Silence, Avoiding People.

Always Stalling, Always Postponing!

Avoiding Stress And Procrastinating.

Avoiding Serious Assignments... Pest!

Adult Successfully Avoiding Projects.

Absolutely Snail's Activity Pace

Always Seeking Alternatives? Priority?

Asleep, Snoring, Awake, Pronto!

Something to consider my friends...

Chapter 3:

Quote-Worthy in 60 Seconds: Uncover Your Hidden Talent

MONEY WITH AMY SERIES

THE PROFITABLE ENTREPRENEUR:
16 Ways to Retrain Entrepreneurs
Using Mindset, Time Management,
Leveraging Your Resources and
Enjoying More Business Travel Inexpensively

Do you read other professionals, insightful, enthusiastic, wise, thought-provoking, humous, memorable, or timeless quotes, and you think to yourself "I could never do that!"

What if I knew you were wrong?

If I could teach you to be quote worthy in less than one minute, would you be willing to learn how and try it right now?

Let me show you one fast and uncomplicated way to do it.

I saw a brilliant take on this from Susan Harrow, a well-known wiz at generating public relations (PR for short). I believe in giving credit where credit is due.

Sometime ago, Susan began a "Fave Quote Friday" series.

Her brilliant idea was to take a meaningful quote she loves, and resonated with, then put a bit of a commentary on it to give her a new personal quote with her own outlook and insight wrapped up in it.

As a result, Susan has her own inspiring quote to share with her audience.

She is a clever and resourceful lady. Don't you agree?

Here is one of my favorite quotes.

"20 years from now you will be more disappointed by the things that you did not do than by the ones you did do. So, throw off the bow lines. Sail away from the safe harbor. Catch the trade winds in your sails. Explore, dream, and discover.

Mark Twain

Here is what I heard in this quote that I quickly penned for this publication to have my own quote worthy version:

"Why are you waiting for another 20 years to pass before you live your dreams? Today is your opportunity to put in motion the steps to live the life you always dreamed of."

Amy Rose Herrick

Please share your favorite quote attributing it to the original author, and your quote inspired by it.

Section Two – What You are Not Doing, You Should Be Doing In Any Business

Chapter 4:

30 Timeless Business Lessons Playing Monopoly Gave Us

MONEY WITH AMY SERIES

THE PROFITABLE ENTREPRENEUR:
16 Ways to Retrain Entrepreneurs
Using Mindset, Time Management,
Leveraging Your Resources and
Enjoying More Business Travel Inexpensively

I saw a brilliant post on Facebook about lessons that we can take away from the game of Monopoly. I like to give credit where credit is due. Thank you, Casey D. Eberhart for posting this and sparking my literary creativity today!

Casey included a list of eight potential business lessons in his post. I added twenty-two more relevant lessons I could see when looking at this game from a fresh perspective.

#1 Always be patient.

#2 The most expensive asset is not the best.

#3 Focus on cash flow.

#4 Always keep some cash on hand. (Can I hear an "Amen" to that one?)

#5 Your location matters.

#6 Diversify your investments.

#7 Negotiating is a powerful skill.

#8 Having passive income is key.

Now I will add my twenty-two additional unique business lessons we can learn from playing Monopoly from my viewpoint.

#9 Be ready to take a chance now and then.

#10 Remember to circle back to where you started from, to reaffirm the direction to which you are headed.

#11 There are times in your life when your financial destiny will be changed quickly with what amounts to the roll of the dice. Keep playing anyway to see what happens.

#12 In real life you cannot get out of jail free without any consequences.

#13 The token that you select to play with today, to represent who you are for a fleeting time, can be changed in the future when it no longer fits who you are

#14 Do not forget to regularly invest in your community.

#15 Be prepared to stick it out all the way to the very end, even if it takes longer than you initially expected.

#16 Choose well and enjoy the people you choose to surround yourself with.

#17 In life, just like when you are playing Monopoly, rarely will there be a lot of shortcuts along the way.

#18 Never forget to pay all business and personal taxes promptly!

#19 Creativity is like a faucet. Turn on the tap frequently,

#20 When you are not in the driver's seat, sit back and enjoy the ride.

#21 Adaptability is crucial in a changing business landscape.

#22 Timing is everything when making strategic moves.

#23 Anticipate and plan for unexpected expenses.

#24 Understand the value of building relationships.

#25 Assess your risks and potential rewards before making major decisions.

#26 Learn from your mistakes and adjust your strategy accordingly.

#27 Embrace the competition and strive to outperform your rivals.

#28 Develop a long-term vision and set clear goals for your business.

#29 Keep a close eye on industry trends and adapt your offerings accordingly.

#30 Acquiring and leveraging assets can give you a competitive edge.

If you are a business owner, you may decide to hang a Monopoly board on your wall as a consistent reminder of your earliest forays into being an entrepreneur and the lessons the game can still teach you.

Chapter 5:

Financial Statements Made Simple

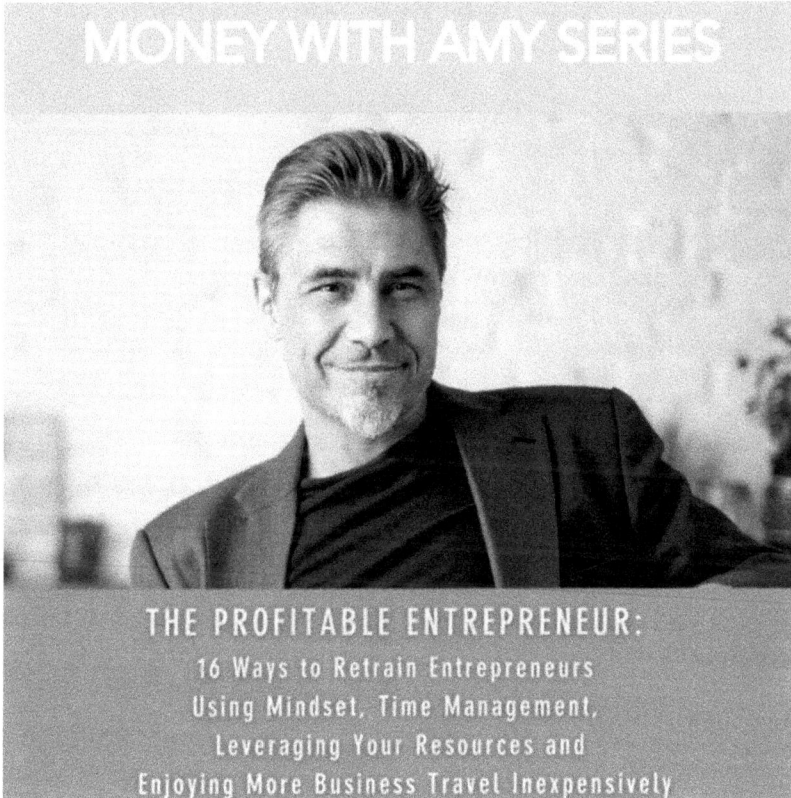

MONEY WITH AMY SERIES

THE PROFITABLE ENTREPRENEUR:
16 Ways to Retrain Entrepreneurs
Using Mindset, Time Management,
Leveraging Your Resources and
Enjoying More Business Travel Inexpensively

Financial statements may sound like a big, confusing thing, but do not worry! We are here to help you understand them, just like you are a clever 5-year-old. Financial statements are like special reports that tell us how a company or a person is doing with their money. They are important because they can help us make better decisions. So, let us dive in and learn together!

What Are Financial Statements?

Imagine you have a piggy bank where you keep your coins. Now, think of a company or a person having their own piggy bank, but it is much, much bigger. Financial statements are like a way to peek inside that big piggy bank and see how much money is in there and how it is being used.

The Three Important Statements:

There are three main types of financial statements: the balance sheet, the income statement, and the cash flow statement. Each one tells us something different about the money in the piggy bank.

a) Balance Sheet:

The balance sheet is like a snapshot of what is in the piggy bank at a certain moment. It shows us how much money the company or person has (their assets) and what they owe to others (their liabilities). It is like counting the coins and knowing if they have more or less than before. I will say it is also a sheet of lies in a couple of areas. Whoa, I said it contains lies?!?!? Yes, lies. Let me explain that. The value of the property, real estate, or cars for example, is based on the cost at the time of purchase, less accumulated depreciation, not current market value. Current market value can be quite different.

b) Income Statement:

The income statement tells us how the company or person earned their money and how much they spent. It is like looking at the piggy bank and seeing how many coins they put in and how many they took out. This statement helps us know if they made a profit (earned more than they spent) or a loss (spent more than they earned).

c) Cash Flow Statement:

The cash flow statement is all about tracking the money that goes in and out of the piggy bank over a period. It shows us where the money comes from (like customers paying for things) and where it goes (like paying for expenses or buying new things). It helps us understand if the company or person has enough money to keep things going.

Why Are Financial Statements Important?

Financial statements are like secret codes that help us understand how a company or person is doing financially. They are important because they can help us make smart decisions. For example, if we want to invest in a company or buy something from them, we can look at their financial statements to see if they are doing well or not. We can also use these statements to compare different companies and see which one is doing the best.

> **"I call it the Rule of Three. If you read a company's financial statements three times, and you still cannot figure out how they make their money, that is usually for a reason."** *James Chanos*

Financial statements may seem like a grown-up thing, but with a little explanation, even a 5-year-old can understand them. Remember, they are like special reports about money, and they help us make better decisions. So, the next time you hear about financial statements, think of them as a tool to peek into a giant piggy bank and understand how what is inside is being used.

If you want to learn more and dive deeper into the fascinating world of financial statements, I invite you to book a 15-minute consultation with me free! Let us explore together and answer any questions you may have. To schedule a 15-minute Zoom based discovery call to discuss becoming a client for comprehensive financial planning or business profit building assistance at:

https://calendly.com/amyroseherrick/15min

Chapter 6:

Five Methods to Value Your Mailing List for Online Business Success: How to quickly determine the value of each email address on any mailing list for purchase or sale.

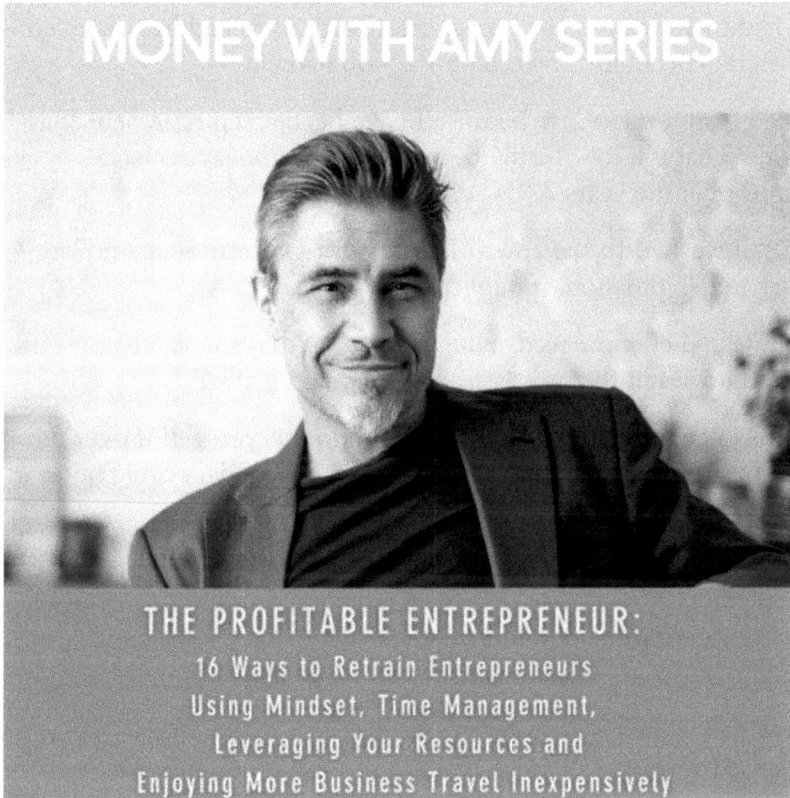

MONEY WITH AMY SERIES

THE PROFITABLE ENTREPRENEUR:
16 Ways to Retrain Entrepreneurs
Using Mindset, Time Management,
Leveraging Your Resources and
Enjoying More Business Travel Inexpensively

An electronic based mailing list is an often undervalued, forgotten and a difficult to value business asset for any business with an online component. This list allows businesses to directly communicate with their customers and prospects, providing a more personalized and targeted experience.

We all have mailing lists of some variation. They are a living organism, always changing.

My team and I recently did a huge third-party email verification and compilation process. I pulled emails from every place I could think of. I had them make a large main list. CRM's, email addresses saved on different accounts, my cell phone, you name it.

I pulled from everywhere because I have been an entrepreneur for decades. That is a lot of data to possess as my endeavors have changed over the years .

For us, it was worth the effort. The cost for verification, compiling the list and elimination of duplicates was small.

The time and energy saved, a huge return on that enabled us to shift some strategies in the most streamlined way possible!

You may need to take a deep breath and do this yourself if over the years you have engaged different platforms where data could be stored.

All this leads to determining the value of a single mailing list can be a challenging task, as there are many factors to consider. In this article, we will explore some potential methods for valuing a mailing list for an online business endeavor.

I know you want the answer first, I will give it to you in the condensed version, but please read to the end for some other considerations on list valuations.

Show me the money when you want to sell me your list!

When it comes to the value of a mailing list, it is important to consider the potential revenue that the list can generate will be a pricing consideration of any buyer. The value of a mailing list is typically measured by the return on investment (ROI) that it generates for the business.

Here are some examples of how I would look at the value of a list for purchase to grow my own marketing reach.

#1

For example, if a mailing list of 10,000 subscribers generates $10,000 in revenue for the business annually, the value of each email address on the list could be stated as $1 at most. They cannot provide any average sale data. I may be willing to pay up to $10,000 for it if I thought I could get my money back and increase sales above this amount. A list this size would not incur significant costs to maintain or integrate.

#2

If a different 10,000 address list generates $10,000 a month, or $120,000 a year in gross revenue, with the average sale of $250 equating to around 480 sales a year, it has a 0.048% engagement level. It could be considered the highest valuation to be $12 per email address. I may be willing to pay up to $120,000 for it if I thought I could get my money back and increase sales above this amount. A list this size would not incur significant costs to maintain or integrate.

#3

If I had a list, I would consider 923,000 subscribers, and it generates $42,100 a year in gross revenue, no stats to go with it to break down engagement percentages were possible. I would value it at only 0.0456 cents per name at the highest level. I may be reluctantly willing to pay up to $42,100 for it if I thought I could get my money back and increase sales above this amount in a reasonable period.

On this one, I would need to weigh the time involved to manage a list of this size and the increased ongoing operating costs of maintaining the database over time as additional acquisition costs to decide if this large unengaged list was worth owning.

#4

If I had a list of 2,310,000 subscribers, and it generates $225,000 a year in gross revenues on the table, I would look at it no differently than a small list for viability. This one documents for me the average sale is $65. That is around 3,461 sales a year. Engagement is low at 0.00149%.

On the high end, I would value it at only 0.097 cents per name.

I may be reluctantly willing to pay up to $225,000 for it if I thought I could get my money back and increase sales above this amount in a reasonable period.

On this one, I would have to carefully weigh the time involved to manage a list of this size and the increased ongoing operating costs of maintaining the database over time as additional acquisition costs to decide if this large list was worth owning.

Showing your potential buyer where the value is when you want to sell your list!

If you own a list, you can use the same methodology I used in the prior section to determine what the value of your list could be to a potential buyer.

If you do not have a method of tracking the average sale and engagement percentages you could produce and show a buyer proving results over time, get one in place now to have facts to back up your offering price.

Does your list size matter the most?

I do not think size is as important as value when contemplating this valuation issue.

For targeted niches, you may not need a large list when you have active buyers and consistent repeat sales from a loyal audience to increase the value of each email address you own.

Cluttered lists that do not include potential buyers within your target audience are not worth anything to your bottom line.

They clutter up your list and increase your carrying costs.

Calculate the Cost of Acquisition

The first method for valuing a mailing list is to calculate the cost of acquisition. This involves adding up the cost of all the marketing and advertising campaigns that were used to acquire the email addresses on the list.

This method is especially useful if the business purchased a mailing list from a third-party provider, as it can help determine whether the purchase was a worthwhile investment as you measure the return on your investment over time.

In my analysis, to calculate the cost of acquisition, the business must also factor in any labor or resources used to integrate the lists and to create the innovative marketing campaigns to evaluate and engage this audience.

Determine the Lifetime Value of Customers

The lifetime value of customers is another key factor to consider when valuing a mailing list.

This metric measures the total revenue generated by a customer over their lifetime with the business.

By analyzing the lifetime value of customers, businesses can determine the potential revenue that the mailing list could generate in the future.

For example, if the business sells products or services that are regularly purchased, such as a subscription service, the lifetime value of customers may be higher, making the mailing list more valuable.

Compare to Industry Averages

Finally, businesses can value their mailing list by comparing it to industry averages.

This involves researching industry benchmarks for metrics such as open and click-through rates, conversion rates, and lifetime value of customers.

By comparing the mailing list metrics to industry averages, businesses can determine how their mailing list stacks up against their competitors.

This can provide valuable insights into the mailing list's potential for generating revenue and help businesses determine its overall value.

Average sale price per email address for purchased broad based mailing lists offers.

Determining the average sale price per email address for mailing lists can be a challenging task, as there are many factors that can impact the value of a mailing list.

The cost per email address can vary significantly depending on the quality of the list, the size of the list, the industry or niche, and the purpose of the mailing list.

Some mailing lists may be available for purchase from third-party providers, while others may be built organically through a business's own marketing efforts.

Mailing lists that are purchased from third-party providers can range in price from a few cents per email address to several dollars per email address, depending on the quality of the list and the size of the purchase they are offering.

However, it is important to note that purchasing a mailing list is not always the most effective way to build a high-quality list of email addresses.

Scrub your list.

At the time of purchase, I would independently scrub any list if I bought one before using it to make certain I got what I paid for.

I would expect and have as a part of the purchase agreement to get a refund on all unusable addresses in my purchased list.

Make sure to negotiate and have in writing what the refund policy will be on these third-party reports with unusable email addresses on your purchased list. Or withhold a portion of the purchase price until the scrubbed list can be presented to adjust final purchase prices.

You may find that you already have some email addresses on your list as duplicates. Unless you negotiate that you will not pay for duplicates already in your database, you will pay for them a second time.

The value of a mailing list depends on a variety of factors, including the quality of the subscribers, the engagement and interest of the subscribers, the effectiveness of the email marketing campaigns, and the potential for generating revenue.

As such, it can be difficult to determine an average sale price across the board per email address for mailing lists, as the value of each list can vary significantly.

By carefully analyzing these factors, using the analysis steps given to you above, businesses can make informed decisions about how to leverage their mailing list to grow their business valuations and saleable assets.

Chapter 7:

Cybersecurity for Every Business: Why a WISP is Essential

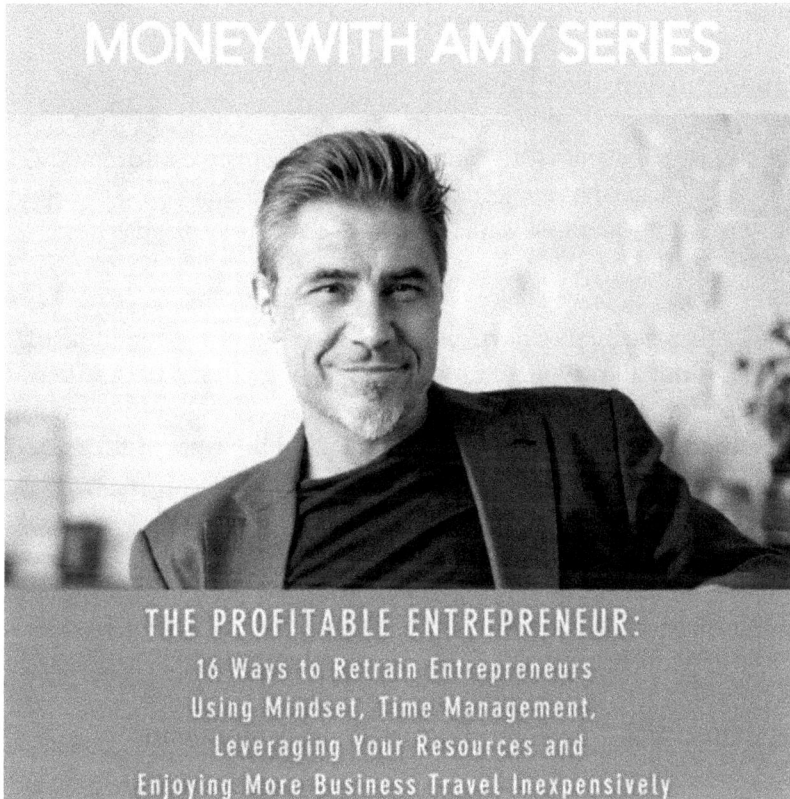

MONEY WITH AMY SERIES

THE PROFITABLE ENTREPRENEUR:
16 Ways to Retrain Entrepreneurs
Using Mindset, Time Management,
Leveraging Your Resources and
Enjoying More Business Travel Inexpensively

In today's digital age, information security has become a critical concern for businesses of all sizes. Whether you own a tax or accounting business who will be most familiar with this type of protocol, or any other type of enterprise, implementing a Written Information Security Program (WISP) is crucial.

A WISP is a comprehensive plan that outlines the measures and protocols necessary to protect sensitive information from unauthorized access or breaches. This article will discuss five reasons why every business, including sole proprietors, should have a WISP and what such a plan should include.

Safeguarding Sensitive Data:

Businesses manage and store various forms of sensitive information, such as customer data, financial records, and proprietary information. A WISP helps protect this valuable data from unauthorized access, misuse, or theft.

It is a fact that businesses have employee turnover for a multitude of reasons. Do not allow yourself to be an easy mark in the back office. By implementing security measures and best practices, businesses can mitigate the risk of data breaches and safeguard the trust of their customers and stakeholders.

> *Statistics: According to a study by the National Cyber Security Alliance, 60% of small businesses close within six months of a cyberattack. The average cost of a data breach for small businesses is approximately $200,000.*

Compliance with Legal and Regulatory Requirements:

Many industries have legal and regulatory requirements pertaining to data protection and privacy. By having a WISP, businesses can ensure they comply with these obligations.

Are you aware that the General Data Protection Regulation (GDPR) in Europe and the California Consumer Privacy Act (CCPA) have stringent requirements for data protection and privacy? They do. A

WISP helps businesses meet these standards and avoid costly penalties for non-compliance.

Sole Proprietors and WISP:

Even if you operate as a sole proprietor without any employees, having a WISP is still crucial.

As a sole proprietor, you may oversee sensitive customer information, financial data, or proprietary information.

A WISP ensures that you have a structured approach to protecting this information from potential risks. It demonstrates your commitment to data security and can help establish trust with your customers.

Mitigating Financial Loss:

Information security breaches can have severe financial implications for businesses.

The costs associated with data breaches include legal fees, regulatory fines, customer compensation, damage to reputation, and the expenses involved in recovering and securing compromised systems.

By having a WISP in place, businesses can reduce the likelihood and impact of these incidents, potentially saving significant financial resources and avoiding a closure that is a direct result of a data breach that could have been avoided.

Protecting Business Continuity:

In the event of a data breach, businesses may experience significant disruptions, leading to operational downtime and loss of revenue.

By implementing a WISP, businesses can proactively identify vulnerabilities and implement measures to prevent or mitigate potential breaches.

This initiative-taking approach helps maintain business continuity and minimizes the impact on operations, allowing for a quicker recovery while protecting the business bottom line.

What Should a WISP Plan Include?

A comprehensive WISP plan should address the following key components:

Risk Assessment: Identify potential threats, vulnerabilities, and risks to your business's information security.

Security Policies and Procedures: Outline specific policies and procedures to protect sensitive information, including access controls, password management, employee training, and incident response protocols.

Data Classification and Handling: Define how diverse types of data should be classified, stored, transmitted, and disposed of securely.

Physical and Environmental Security: Address physical security measures, such as restricted access to sensitive areas and secure storage for physical documents.

Vendor Management: Establish guidelines for selecting and managing third-party vendors who have access to your business's data.

Regardless of the nature or size of your business, implementing a Written Information Security Program (WISP) is crucial for protecting sensitive information, complying with legal requirements, mitigating financial losses, ensuring business continuity, and building trust with customers.

Section Three-
Your Time = Money:
Why Owner Efficiency Is Essential!

Chapter 8:

"Crunching the Numbers: Calculating Your Net Worth in Minutes"

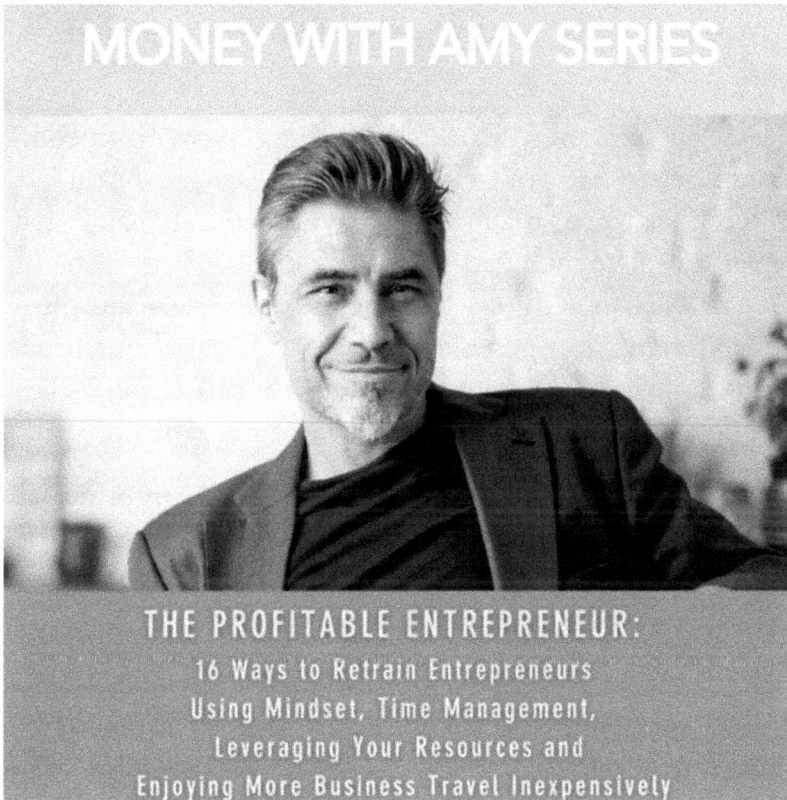

MONEY WITH AMY SERIES

THE PROFITABLE ENTREPRENEUR:
16 Ways to Retrain Entrepreneurs
Using Mindset, Time Management,
Leveraging Your Resources and
Enjoying More Business Travel Inexpensively

Calculating your net worth is a quick and painless process once you understand the basic steps.

Briefly, the process involves adding up all your assets (what you own) and subtracting your liabilities (what you owe). Here are the basic steps to quickly calculate your net worth:

List all your assets that have a value:

This can include your home, car, undeveloped land, business or partnership interests, investments, savings, and retirement accounts to name only a few common asset classes.

The asset accumulation world is changing. Now you need to remember to add your cloud-based assets. Have you considered that your mailing lists have a separate value that you may not have included in your business asset valuation? Websites, Blogs or Podcasts audiences and the revenue streams they generate are assets. What about your domain names and Trademarks value? Crypto currency is an asset. These need to be added to your net worth.

Here are a few more categories you may have forgotten about: Art, a walnut tree grove for wood harvesting in 10 years, and fine jewelry to name a few more to help you include all assets that add to your net worth.

Now it is time to add up the value of all your listed and identified assets. For each asset, determine its current value and add it to the total. I find it helpful to include how you valued the asset to break down what are wild guesses, based on appraisals and valuation formulas used.

Now we list all your liabilities.

This can include big ticket items such as your mortgage, car loans, student loans, credit card debts, any installment arrangements, loas from family members, etc. . You are including all outstanding debt.

Add up the total amount of your liabilities: For each liability, determine the outstanding balance and add it to the total.

Subtract your liabilities from your assets:

Subtract the total amount of your liabilities from the total value of your assets. The result is your net worth.

There is one last step I have suggested for clients to include as footnotes to the net worth calculations for future reference when changes are anticipated within the next 2-5 years that are not normal minor expenses. These have included estimated inheritances in process, but not yet settled. We have listed notes on potential lawsuit settlements that would either add or subtract from your net worth after attorney fees. An expected upcoming liability could include potential child-related expenses such as paying for weddings and college tuition. There have been situations where we needed to include new or increasing financial assistance for aging parents with declining health or long-term care needs. This step is not required, but I find it helpful to see how these will impact wealth over time.

Here is the concise formula for calculating net worth:

Net worth = Total value of assets - Total amount of liabilities

By following these steps, you can quickly calculate your net worth and get a clear understanding of your financial standing now and in the next few years.

Chapter 9:

Dictations are not dead:

They have been repackaged as Speech-to-text" or "Voice-to-text".

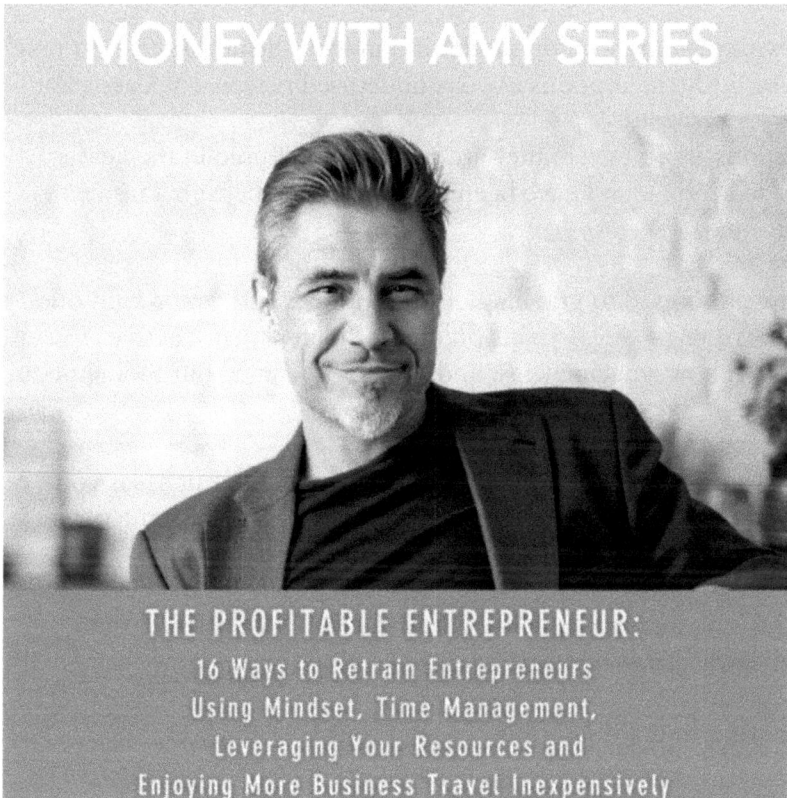

MONEY WITH AMY SERIES

THE PROFITABLE ENTREPRENEUR:
16 Ways to Retrain Entrepreneurs
Using Mindset, Time Management,
Leveraging Your Resources and
Enjoying More Business Travel Inexpensively

You already have a built in 24/7/365 virtual assistant (VA) to save you time and money, and you are not engaging them like you should be.

This VA is never tired, overworked, at home sleeping in a different time zone, or unavailable.

Did I mention they are likely to be already on "staff", but you are not tapping into their talents?

Out with the old dictation model and in with the new speech-to-text" or "voice-to-text" options as your underused personal VA assistant!

Dictations are not dead; they are severely underused in the new upgraded format and have been given a new name with a faster turnaround.

We are all so used to grabbing our cell phones and typing with our thumbs or using our keypads on our computers that we have forgotten how amazingly fast and valuable dictating our thoughts can be.

Using the new text-to-voice model for this old concept saves you tons of time by using the power of your voice instead of the power of your fingers.

Let this sink in, your voice to text 24/7/365 VA is portable and travels with you everywhere.

Your voice to text 24/7/365 VA is efficient.

Your voice to text 24/7/365 VA is free to engage as little or as much as you want without adding another monthly or annual fee.

Your voice to text 24/7/365 VA is faster than you are.

Your voice to text 24/7/365 VA is not perfect, so proof reading is needed.

Have you ever timed how long it takes you to type out responses on your cell phone? It will be much longer than you think. I will not even bring up when *Spellchecker* "helps" you...

At your fingertips you already have options you could and should be using.

Let us go over a few examples where you can evaluate this idea right now with the resources already at your fingertips, even if that have been underused until today:

On my iPhone, I can go to Notes, tap the screen and at the bottom right-hand corner I can tap the microphone and I get talk to text activated. I have learned to hit the space bar between thoughts or paragraphs as I go because it cannot do that for me. Copy, paste and email to me. Free!

On my iPhone, I can go to email, tap the screen and at the bottom right-hand corner I can tap the microphone and I get talk to text activated. I have learned to hit the space bar between thoughts or paragraphs as I go because it cannot do that for me. Free!

On my iPhone I can record a video and send it off for transcribing as another option. May or may not be free.

On Microsoft Word, go to the home tab, look on the right and there is a microphone here too! In fact, I have been dictating much of the content you see here because it is so much faster than me typing it. Free!

Google Docs' built-in Voice Typing feature to convert your speech into text. Open a Google Docs document, go to "Tools" in the top menu, and select "Voice typing" from the dropdown menu.

Click on the microphone icon that appears and start speaking. Your speech will be transcribed into the document in real-time. Free when you already pay for this feature.

Are you a Zoom user? Start a Zoom meeting and enable cloud recording or local recording during the meeting. Conduct your meeting as usual, with participants speaking. After the meeting, Zoom will process the recording, and it will be available to view or download.

To transcribe the meeting, you can use various transcription services or tools, which will convert the audio in the recording to text. Some transcription services allow you to directly upload the Zoom recording for transcription, making the process more streamlined. May or may not be free integrations.

Microsoft Dictate is an add-on for Microsoft Office products, including Word, Outlook, and PowerPoint, which allows you to use voice-to-text functionality. It utilizes the power of Microsoft's speech recognition technology. To use it, you will need to install the "Dictate" add-on from the Microsoft Office Store. Free if you already have this software installed!

Apple Dictation (Mac): If you have a Mac computer, you can use Apple's built-in Dictation feature. Go to System Preferences > Keyboard > Dictation and turn on Dictation.

Press the designated shortcut (by default, it is pressing the Function (fn) key twice) to activate dictation in any text field.

Do you use Searchie? There is a transcription processing option here too included in your fees. Free!

Online Voice-to-Text Tools: There are various online voice-to-text tools available that do not require any software installation. Examples include Speechnotes, Online Dictation, and SpeechTexter, among others. Simply open the website, allow access to your microphone, and start speaking. The tool will transcribe your speech into text.

This is the beginning on voice to text!

How many of these tools do you have access to now?

How many are you using daily?

"Oh Amy, come on use it for what?"

Brain flashes! You are in the middle of doing something and you do not want to stop this project, I use my phone, dictate it, it will go to e-mail, I can find it later.

You need to compose a letter on the run, excellent, dictate it.

Do you want to dictate the steps as you a project step by step to train someone else remotely?

Are you trying to draft an article or blog?

Did you see something that gave you an idea you do not want to forget?

A book?

Give staff or family members detailed instructions on how to manage an emergency.

Are you sick of replying about how you are doing when you or a loved one is sick? Dictate it once, then copy and paste it when kindhearted people ask. Edit as needed on what you share with whom.

Need to share a recipe?

I have families that successfully used dictation services to record priceless oral family history they wanted to share, but it was going to die with them, if it did not get recorded.

We had Dad talk into a tool. All he had to do was to tell stories when he thought of one. When he dictated the story in a speech to text note, they were typed, and they were sent to his daughter by email. She edited and compiled them all.

He could dictate anytime he wanted.

The value of these stories to the family was priceless.

It was inexpensive to get the result they wanted. It was an uncomplicated way to make it happen for everyone.

How could you leverage dictations to increase your profitability?

Are you training your staff or VAs to dictate to save time on the voice to text tools?

Dictations are not dead; they are repackaged as voice-to-text options that are dramatically underused.

Starting today, let us supercharge your productivity with integrating voice-to-text on at least three projects and soon you too will be speaking more and typing less.

If you save a mere 30 minutes a day, five days a week, all year for 10 years in dictating versus typing, you will have another 7,800 minutes a year to do something else with. Amazing!

That is 78,000 minutes or 1,300 hours in 10 years you do not need to type your thoughts.

Chapter 10:

Extra monitors, laptops, and printers/scanners can improve profits

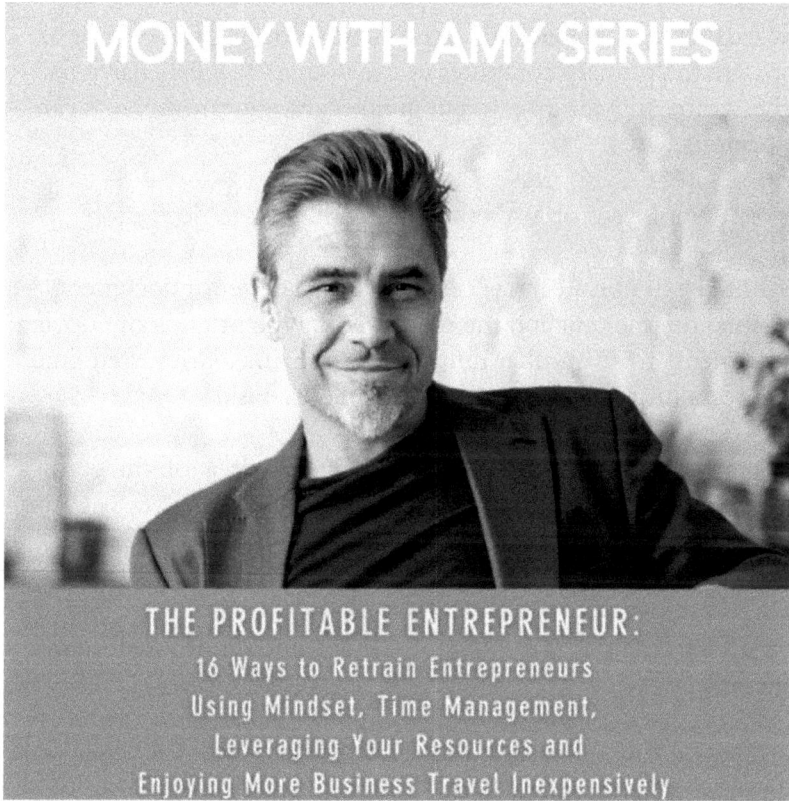

MONEY WITH AMY SERIES

THE PROFITABLE ENTREPRENEUR:
16 Ways to Retrain Entrepreneurs
Using Mindset, Time Management,
Leveraging Your Resources and
Enjoying More Business Travel Inexpensively

Extra monitors, printers, backup laptops or docking stations are not a luxury.

If you are in an office setting, instead of one computer monitor, do you, your staff or VA's need multiple monitors or printers per station to get the job done faster, easier, and with greater accuracy?

A few extra monitors, backup laptops and a docking station when laptops are the primary computer in use is an easy, inexpensive fix and the return on your investment and accuracy improvements can be enormous.

Give your employees or VA's the right tech tools to do the job.

A dedicated extra printer/scanner can allow one set of documents to be scanned on one unit and the employee can be printing or copying off documents from another unit at the same time. No wasted time waiting for a turn at a single unit to complete a task!

If it takes you or an employee an hour longer to do a job three times a week with only one monitor or printer, and this employee is costing you $50 an hour in overhead, can you afford not to spend $200-$400 on technology?

The math tells me this is costing me a huge amount of money and productivity!

$50 an hour x 3 hours a week x 48 work weeks a year = $7,200 a year plus employee frustration to NOT have an extra monitor or printer! In ten years this easy to solve profit eating problem will gobble up $72,000+ of my employees' time!

Now what could we be doing with those 3 hours a week for 48 weeks a year?

That is 144 hours a year we could use the time to do something else to make us more profits.

That is eighteen full working days a year wasted because the employee does not have a second monitor or printer!

Now that you are seeing this through a unique perspective, do not continue to give up almost four weeks of productivity a year, on just this one employee example because you will not invest $200-$400 into needed electronics!

How much more profit could it cost you by not having a needed extra monitor or printer in place now?

Is your problem a computer issues? Here is an easy solution to that one too!

When you are having computer issues, no doubt upsetting you, and wasting your or staff time, how does it affect your attitude?

Stop the insanity! Set it aside, plug in the backup computer to resume your project with ease, a smile on your face.

If you have everything synchronized on the cloud because you pull it out once a month and let it do so if needed, you will lose minutes, not hours of your day because you planned for this moment to happen on your terms.

What do you do with the other one that is misbehaving? You deal with it within the week on your time frame, or you take it to a computer store and let them deal with it.

What is your time an emotional state worth sitting on tech support for three to four hours of your day? Mine is worth a lot compared to handing it off and picking it back up later for a few dollars saving me from hyperventilating or coming close to tears, yes tears from the stress it induces. I am a fixer and wizard at producing all kinds of solutions to problems. Computers are not my area of joy, so why do it?

Let me appeal to your financial side. If you earn $150 an hour, and fooling with a misbehaving computer tech support takes 3 hours, it cost you $450, and you are 4 hours behind on whatever project you were working on when all this started. I doubt the computer store will cost even half that even for stubborn issues. More importantly, they live to do this kind of stuff. We do not!

When did you last replace a computer? Let me tell you a little secret about hard drives told to me by a highly trained, talented, wise computer tech.

> *There are only two types of hard drives in the world. One kind has already failed you. The second is the one that will fail you at an extremely inconvenient time. The one you need to worry about is the one that has not failed yet.*

This means you need to replace your computer and upgrade it before it fails you at an inconvenient time. Usually, because I live in the tropics in the salt air, I anticipate that I am not going to get more than about two or at most three years out of a computer.

I call it the cost of doing business and I use one of the most recently replaced computers as my backup. It is a lot cheaper for me when it comes to my time and money to replace a computer and install all the programs before my old one fails than to drop everything and to deal with it at an inconvenient time.

Let me share a little life lesson with you on this topic.

I attended a professional a conference in Austin TX many years ago. On the plane I am being kind when I am using the word "gentleman" for the angry idiot who upon boarding the plane kept kicking my computer underneath the seat and would not stop when I was trying to get it unjammed from his back kick during boarding. I finally ended up screaming if you will just stop kicking for a moment, I will move the computer. The flight attendant came and asked him to just get out of the seat in front of me for a moment and stand aside. I had the support of the other passengers around me at the time seeing how he was behaving and told her so.

At the hotel when I opened it up and realized it was dented on one corner point. Of course, it would not turn on. Looking at the clock, I ran down to the front desk, where I bribed a hotel employee going home to get me rapidly to a computer store.

I picked out what was on the shelf, paid the salesperson to stay late to get me operational to enable me to have my laptop and work the conference as planned the next day. I was ready to go after staying up half the night loading the needed programs. This was an inconvenient failure event.

My second failure a few years later, less an enraged idiot in the seat in front of me, was in San Diego, CA where I had worked for over 12 hours in airports and planes during a long travel day on various projects on my laptop.

While I was in my hotel room on my buffer day, I got the blue screen of death without warning before all the projects I had worked on had a chance to synchronize on the cloud. Fortunately, I was within walking distance of a computer store and of course I bought one and did it all over again.

The moral of the story is that I now travel everywhere with my primary and a backup computer. This has served me well when on two-week business-oriented cruise my primary computer died on the second day. I merely packed it away, pulled out my backup computer and did not miss a beat.

Second moral of the story: is that when I am working on my computer in an airport or on an airplane, I have a thumb drive with me. I back up everything on the thumb drive as I go in addition to what is saved on my computer. If I ever have a computer failure again, before the work during travel has synchronized, I have my thumb drive ready to go as my Plan B to never lose hours of my efforts again.

On these types of things, I am an adaptive learner, are you?

Section Four – Where Do You Find More Money?

Chapter 11:

Beyond Traditional Financing: Leveraging Self-Directed Retirement Accounts for Business and Rental Property Acquisition

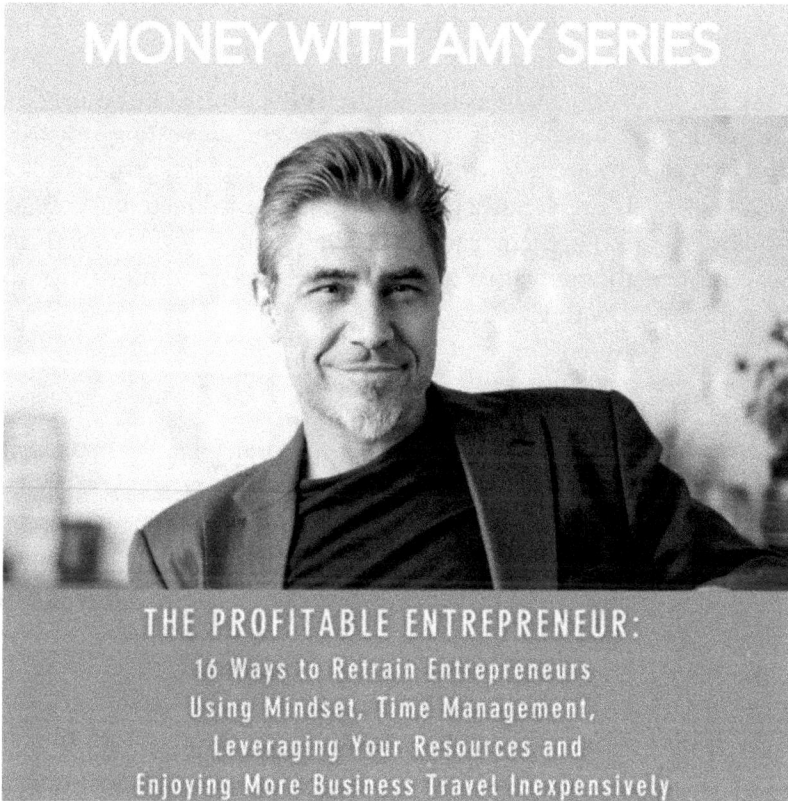

MONEY WITH AMY SERIES

THE PROFITABLE ENTREPRENEUR:
16 Ways to Retrain Entrepreneurs
Using Mindset, Time Management,
Leveraging Your Resources and
Enjoying More Business Travel Inexpensively

A self-directed IRA or self-directed Roth IRA is an investment account that allows individuals to invest in a wide range of assets beyond traditional stocks, bonds, and mutual funds.

With a self-directed IRA or self-directed Roth IRA, investors can use their retirement funds to own businesses or rental properties.

However, there are several mistakes to avoid when using these types of accounts for non-traditional asset building funding resources.

Mistake #1: Failing to Understand the Rules and Regulations

One of the biggest mistakes individuals make when investing in a self-directed IRA or self-directed Roth IRA is failing to understand the rules and regulations. There are strict guidelines for self-directed accounts, and failure to follow them can result in penalties and fees. It is important to collaborate with a qualified custodian or administrator to ensure compliance with all regulations.

Mistake #2: Not Doing Enough Research

Another mistake that investors make is not doing enough research before investing in a business or rental property. It is essential to conduct due diligence on any investment opportunity to determine its potential profitability and risks. Investors should also consult with a financial advisor or tax professional to assess the tax implications of any investment.

Mistake #3: Mixing Personal and Retirement Funds

Investors should never mix personal funds with their retirement funds. Doing so can disqualify the account from its tax-advantaged status, resulting in penalties and fees. It is essential to keep personal and retirement funds separate.

Mistake #4: Failing to Properly Document Transactions

Another mistake to avoid is failing to document all transactions and investments made with the self-directed IRA or self-directed Roth IRA.

Proper documentation is essential for tax reporting purposes and can help avoid any potential audit issues.

Mistake #5: Failing to Pay Required Fees

Lastly, investors should not overlook the fees associated with a self-directed IRA or self-directed Roth IRA. These accounts require more administrative work, and therefore, have higher fees than traditional retirement accounts. It is essential to pay all required fees to maintain the account's status and avoid any penalties.

Mistake #6: Failing to have enough liquidity in the account for expenses

Every expense, let me repeat that so it sinks in, every expense must be paid from the account. If all the assets are invested in non-liquid assets, and there is no cash to pay expenses when they occur, you are headed for trouble and you could end up violating rule #3, never mix your personal and retirement funds in an endeavor.

On average, the annual fee to maintain the record keeping for a self-directed IRA or self-directed Roth IRA can vary widely based on the number and complexity of assets within the account. I have been aware of fees ranging from a nominal $250 to over $5,000 annually with a large, complex rental heavy portfolio within the self-directed account. However, fees can vary widely depending on the custodian or administrator chosen.

It is also important to note that losses in a self-directed IRA or self-directed Roth IRA are not treated the same as losses in non-qualified accounts for income tax purposes. Losses in a self-directed IRA or self-directed Roth IRA cannot be used to offset gains outside the account. Therefore, it is essential to carefully consider any investment opportunity before committing retirement funds.

In **conclusion**, a self-directed IRA or self-directed Roth IRA can be an excellent way to invest in businesses or rental properties. It is important to avoid the mistakes mentioned above and work with a qualified custodian or administrator to ensure compliance with all regulations. By doing so, investors can maximize the potential benefits of these accounts while minimizing the risks.

It is important to note that the IRS prohibits self-dealing in a self-directed IRA or self-directed Roth IRA. This means that the account owner cannot use the account to benefit themselves or any disqualified persons. Disqualified persons include the account owner's spouse, parents, children, and other family members, as well as any business entities in which the account owner owns at least 50% of the voting stock.

This means that it is generally not allowable for an individual to work for a business that their self-directed IRA or self-directed Roth IRA owns, as doing so would constitute self-dealing. Additionally, any income or benefits received from a business owned by the IRA must flow back into the IRA and cannot be used for personal use.

There are some exceptions to this rule. For example, an individual may be able to work for a business owned by their IRA if they are not receiving any compensation for their services, and the work they are performing is strictly voluntary. Additionally, a self-directed IRA or self-directed Roth IRA may invest in a publicly traded company, and the account owner may own shares of the company and work for it without any issues.

It is important to consult with a tax professional or financial advisor to fully understand the rules and regulations surrounding self-directed IRAs and self-directed Roth IRAs. Violating the rules regarding self-dealing can result in significant penalties and fees and could jeopardize the tax-advantaged status of the account.

Like working for a business owned by a self-directed IRA or self-directed Roth IRA, it is generally not allowable for an individual to perform handyperson services on a rental property owned by their retirement account and pay themselves for those services. This would also be considered self-dealing, as the account owner would be using the account to directly benefit themselves.

It is essential to keep in mind that the primary purpose of a self-directed IRA or self-directed Roth IRA is to invest for retirement, and any investments made should be done so with that goal in mind.

Using the account to generate personal income, either through working for a business owned by the account or performing handyperson services on a rental property, would violate the IRS's rules against self-dealing.

If there are repairs or maintenance that need to be done on a rental property owned by a self-directed retirement account, it is important to hire a third-party contractor to perform the work. The account owner cannot perform the work themselves and pay themselves for those services. Any income or fees received from the rental property must flow back into the IRA or Roth IRA account.

As always, it is crucial to consult with a tax professional or financial advisor to understand the specific rules and regulations governing self-directed retirement accounts. Violating the rules against self-dealing can result in significant penalties and fees and could jeopardize the tax-advantaged status of the account.

For many investors, holding different assets as a part of their overall retirement portfolio outside of the usual cash, stocks and mutual funds is an extremely attractive alternative asset class when managed well.

Chapter 12:

How it is possible to earn 4.8% on just $3,000 or 6% on $10,000?

MONEY WITH AMY SERIES

THE PROFITABLE ENTREPRENEUR:
16 Ways to Retrain Entrepreneurs
Using Mindset, Time Management,
Leveraging Your Resources and
Enjoying More Business Travel Inexpensively

If your bank is charging you monthly service fees because you do not maintain a minimum pre-set balance, you are throwing profits away.

To eliminate a $12 minimum fee recently all we had to do was put $3,000 in the account and leave it there.

Leaving that $3,000 in the account no matter what saved $12 a month x 12 months = $144 we did not need to pay anymore.

$3,000 x 4.8% interest would be $144.

That little bit of base padding in the business account is like earning 4.8% on my $3,000 deposit.

Try getting that kind of tax-free return on $3,000 anywhere else right now consistently!

> *$144 a year is not a lot, but in 10 years it is another $1,440 in profit I get to keep for a one-time action.*

What if it required a $10,000 minimum account balance to eliminate $50 a month in fees? That would be $600 a year in saved fees. That is like earning 6% tax free on your $10,000.

In this second example, it is a straightforward way to add perhaps $6,000 to your profits in ten years.

Is it worth your time today to see where you are throwing your profits away on unnecessary bank fees?

Is it worth staff time to do the research on this potential profit increase to your bottom line?

If it takes staff one hour to make the calls, identify a solution and for you to authorize the transfer of funds this can be a very profitable hour spent with long-term positive results.

Chapter 13:

Stop bartering unprofitable items.

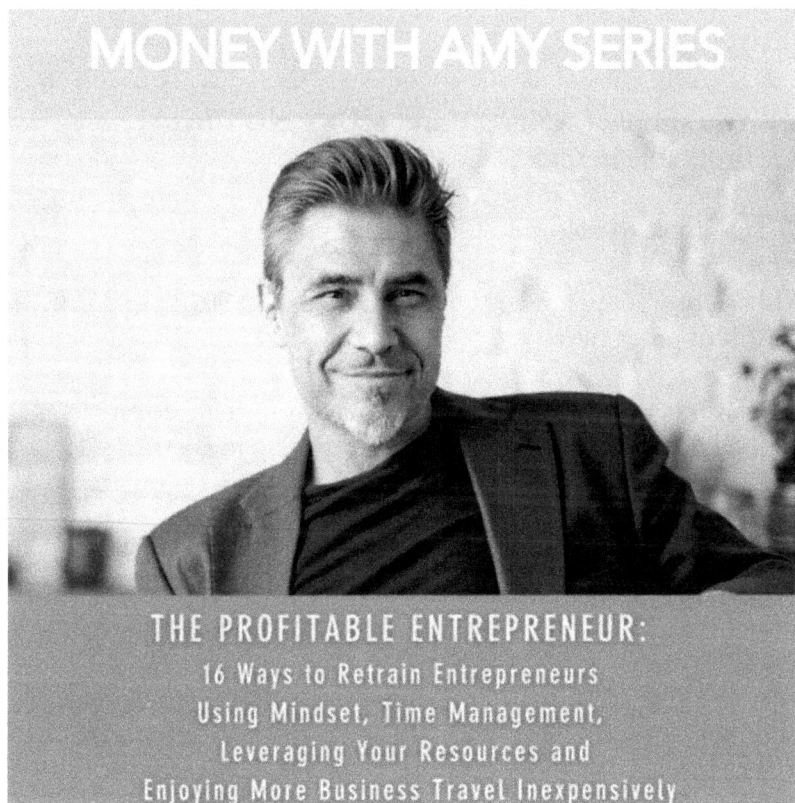

MONEY WITH AMY SERIES

THE PROFITABLE ENTREPRENEUR:
16 Ways to Retrain Entrepreneurs
Using Mindset, Time Management,
Leveraging Your Resources and
Enjoying More Business Travel Inexpensively

Whenever there are pros, there are always going to be cons. Let me tell you a little bit about my personal experience with the Bartering Networks where I saw others fall into profit-reducing traps that they could have avoided.

You need to watch out for including the cost of the trading transaction fees in your sell of items in this manner.

Let me zero in on this point.

> **You simply CANNOT and MUST NOT barter non-profitable items.**

An easy example to help you visualize this point:

If you barter something for $100 and your cost is $90, there is only $10 worth of profit here.

But if your transaction fees when you spend your trade dollars in an established bartering network are 12%, it is going to cost you $12 in cash to sell the items, and you just lost $2 in the process on a $100 sale.

A $2 loss is not much but consider bartering items with losses in high volumes over a series of transactions could cost you plenty.

A larger sale, just add zeros to the above example, may have a larger deficit effect.

These kinds of money-losing transactions do not make sense and can ruin your bottom line.

If you understand the way the membership and transaction fees impact your profits using this type of network, and stay selective on what you barter, or what you are willing to barter, you can use this system to end up with a profit at the end of the transaction.

The other thing you need to consider is that bartering fees in established networks must be paid for in cash each month when billed.

When you run up a bartering bill, then you need to be able to pay for that when the bill comes due and plan accordingly, in cash.

Do not barter more than you can afford to. Barter is different from cash in the bank in your checking account.

If you do not use your barter balances, or the account is idle for a period, you will still generally be required to pay a monthly membership fee until your bartering credits are spent.

Your balance may be idle because you do not have anything that you want to purchase right now, or you are accumulating barter dollars for a single large purchase. The choice is up to you.

Now if you can barter an item including the barter fees at a profit, now you may have another viable way to increase your profits that is untapped at present and open the doors to a new set of buyers to build relationships with.

Here is an easy-to-follow worksheet on the following page to help you decide if bartering an item or service increases or decreases your bottom-line profits.

EXERCISE: Is a barter transaction profitable for you to consider?

Hard cost of the item you will barter

$_____

Trading fee to sell item

+_____

Trading fee to purchase another item

+_____

Monthly trading maintenance fee

+_____

Total hard cost of the transaction

$_____

VS

Value of the barter in your account

$_____

Gain or loss from barter transaction
for this product or service   +/-_____

Decision time:
Proceed with the Barter to make a profit: YES OR NO

Section Five- Secrets To Travel For Less Like the Pros

Chapter 14:

Ten Secrets to Using SkyScanner for Budget Friendly International Travel

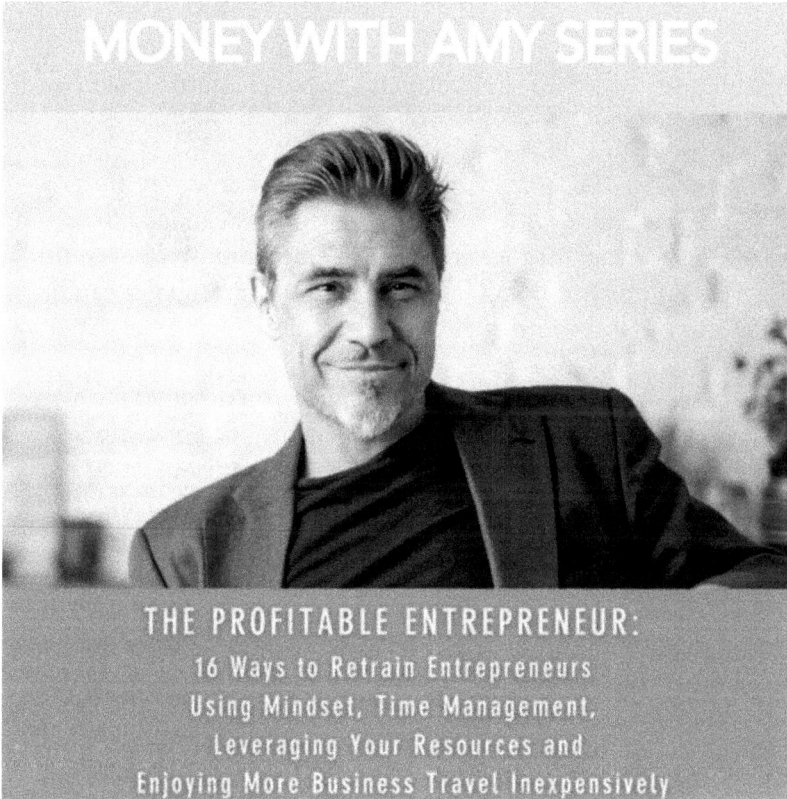

MONEY WITH AMY SERIES

THE PROFITABLE ENTREPRENEUR:
16 Ways to Retrain Entrepreneurs
Using Mindset, Time Management,
Leveraging Your Resources and
Enjoying More Business Travel Inexpensively

Traveling internationally is a dream for many, but it often comes with a hefty price tag. However, with the right tools and techniques, it is possible to plan a budget-friendly international trip.

One such tool that can help you find affordable flights is SkyScanner.

Here are ten secrets of using SkyScanner to travel internationally on a budget:

1. Be flexible with your travel dates: SkyScanner allows you to search for flights across an entire month or even the entire year. Being flexible with your travel dates can help you find cheaper flights.

2. Use the "Everywhere" feature: If you do not have a specific destination in mind, use the "Everywhere" feature to find the cheapest flights to various destinations. Will you travel to Ecuador, Thailand, Costa Rica, Portugal, or Iceland for your next vacay?

3. Set up price alerts: If you have a specific destination in mind, set up price alerts on SkyScanner. This feature will notify you when the flight prices drop, allowing you to book at a lower price.

4. Use the "Map" feature: The "Map" feature on SkyScanner allows you to see the cheapest flights to different destinations on a map. This can help you choose a destination that fits your budget.

5. Consider connecting flights: Connecting flights are often cheaper than direct flights. Use the "Add nearby airports" feature on SkyScanner to search for connecting flights from nearby airports only if this is workable for you.

6. Book in advance: Booking your flight in advance can help you save money. SkyScanner shows you the cheapest flights across a range of dates, so you can find the best time to book.

7. Be open to alternative routes: Sometimes, taking an alternative route or a longer layover can save you money. Use the "Stops" feature on SkyScanner to explore alternative routes.

8. Choose the right time of day: Flying at unpopular times of the day, such as early morning or late at night, can be cheaper. Use the "Time of Day" feature on SkyScanner to find the cheapest flights.

9. Use the "Price Graph" feature: The "Price Graph" feature on SkyScanner allows you to see how flight prices change over time. This can help you choose the best time to book your flight.

10. Sign up for the SkyScanner newsletter: The SkyScanner newsletter includes travel deals and discounts that can help you save money on your international trip.

SkyScanner is an excellent tool for finding affordable flights for your international trip.

By using these ten secrets, you can make the most out of SkyScanner and travel the world on a budget. Happy travels!

Chapter 15:

Ten Money-Saving Tips for Booking Airline Tickets with Google Flights

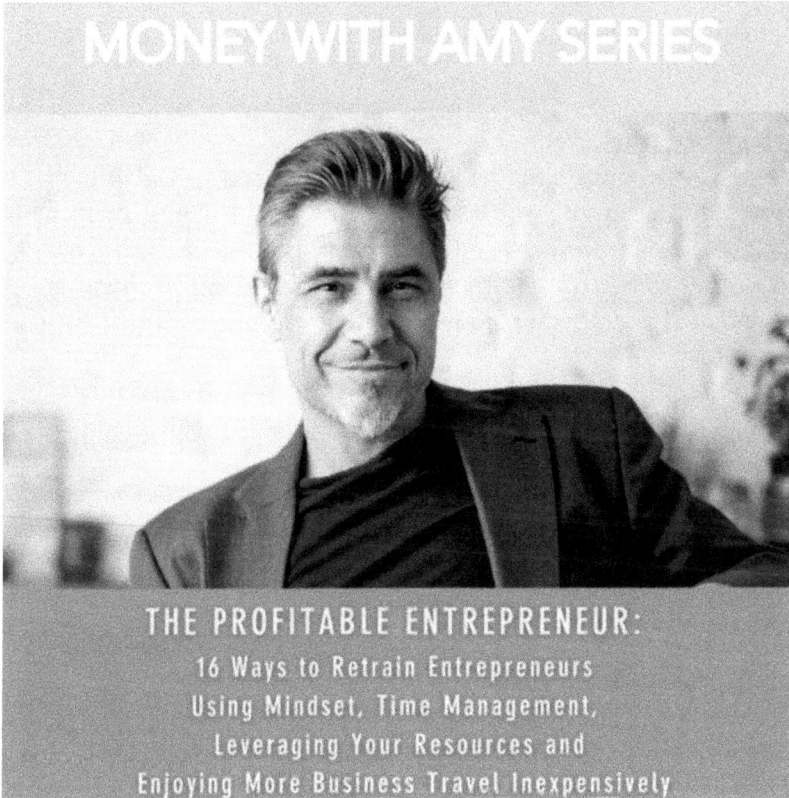

MONEY WITH AMY SERIES

THE PROFITABLE ENTREPRENEUR:
16 Ways to Retrain Entrepreneurs
Using Mindset, Time Management,
Leveraging Your Resources and
Enjoying More Business Travel Inexpensively

When it comes to booking airline tickets, they can be quite expensive if you take the first offer you see, but there are ways to save money using Google Flights that I employ to save money on my travel.

These tips are in addition to any airline credit card benefits or cash back credit card rewards on these travel related purchases I leverage.

Here are my ten tips on how to use Google Flights to save money on your next flight:

Use the price tracker.
You can set up a price alert for a specific flight, and Google Flights will notify you when the price drops.

Some airlines will give you a future flight credit to apply to new flights when the price you paid is more than the current pricing if you ask them to.

I have had this happen on flights where I was able to snag credits twice on the same repriced flight to use another day.

You can only realize these potential windfalls by booking in advance.

The day this article was penned, I have credits to apply to future flights in the amounts of $120.00, $30.60, $48.80, $180, $64, $180, $64, $262.46, and $53.70. They do add up nicely!

Plus, a while back from just a pleasant phone call I was able to receive added back into a family member's account 15,000 miles with one airline in their program.

Those miles will secure a one-way ticket if I book it in advance for less than $15 in processing fees.

My favorite tip must be using the nearby airports feature.

If you have multiple airports in your area, you can use Google Flights to find the cheapest flights from all of them.

Hint: In many cases nearby airports have rental cars much cheaper than major hubs. The combination of a lower cost nearby airport and car rental costs may be attractive to your budget on longer trips for a little inconvenience.

I prefer to use the smaller airports whenever possible. It is so much easier to get through short security lines, return rental cars and the staffing seems to be not as stressed with the smaller crowds to manage.

Be flexible with your travel dates.

Google Flights allows you to see the prices for flights on different days, so you can choose the cheapest day to fly.

Breaking the trip up one way on each leg of your journey can help you spot the best travel day combinations too whether you are coming or going.

1. Use the explore feature. You can search for flights to various places and see the prices for each destination. You can also filter the results by price, duration, and other factors.

2. Book your flight in advance. Booking your flight early can save you a lot of money. Google Flights allows you to see the prices for flights on different dates, so you can book your flight at the cheapest time.

3. Book connecting flights. A flight with a layover can be cheaper than a direct flight. Google Flights allows you to search for flights with layovers and see the prices for each option.

   Depending on your travel needs, a long layover may not be a problem for a remote worker or leisure traveler who is not on a deadline when time is not as important as money.

4. Fly on weekdays. Flying on weekdays is usually cheaper than flying on weekends. Google Flights allows you to search for flights for specific days of the week, so you can find the cheapest day to fly.

5. Use the flexible dates feature. This feature allows you to search for flights within a range of dates. This can help you find the cheapest day to fly.

6. Book during off-peak season. Flying during the off-peak season can save you money. Google Flights allows you to see the prices for flights during different seasons, so you can book your flight at the cheapest time.

7. Use the Google Flights filters. These filters can help you find flights based on specific criteria, such as airline, flight duration, and number of stops.

By following these quick tips, you can save money on your next flight using Google Flights.

Here is a link to Google travel if you are ready to try these tips and tricks right now: https://www.google.com/travel/flights/

Happy travels!

Chapter 16:

Boosting Productivity on Business Trips:

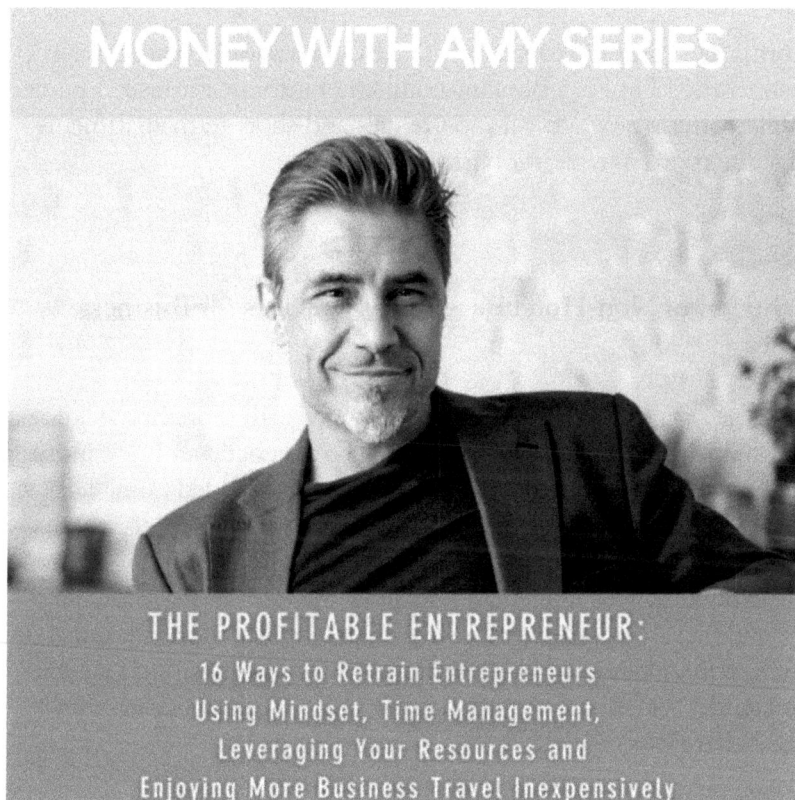

MONEY WITH AMY SERIES

THE PROFITABLE ENTREPRENEUR:
16 Ways to Retrain Entrepreneurs
Using Mindset, Time Management,
Leveraging Your Resources and
Enjoying More Business Travel Inexpensively

Traveling for business can be a stressful experience, especially when it comes to finding a comfortable and convenient place to stay. While hotels are the traditional option for business travelers, there are now several alternatives that offer better amenities and a more homelike experience.

Platforms like Airbnb, HomeAway, VRBO, VacationRentals.com, Trip Advisor owned FlipKey, Booking.com, OneFineStay, Furnished Finder and 9flats offer a range of vacation rentals and short-term apartments that can be more suitable for business trips.

Advantages of Non-Hotel Based Living Spaces for Business Travel

One of the main advantages of renting a space with more homelike living, dining, kitchen, laundry facilities, and extra bedrooms for more than overnight stays is the increase in productivity, added home like conveniences for after hours and the reduction in stress levels.

These extra amenities within the unit allow travelers to feel more at home and be more comfortable, which can lead to a more relaxed and focused mind. Having a full kitchen on site to cook meals and facilities to do laundry while on the road can also save time and money, which can be beneficial for a business trip where time management is crucial.

Another benefit of using vacation rental platforms instead of hotels is the potential to save on lodging costs. Depending on the location and length of stay, a vacation rental can be a more affordable, spacious option than a hotel. This could offset the need or create the excess funds to pay for a rental car in some locations, which could save even more money on overall travel expenses and reduce stress seeking rides on demand.

Safety Features

When selecting accommodations, personal safety features should also be considered. Platforms like Airbnb and HomeAway allow users to filter search results by safety features such as smoke detectors, carbon monoxide detectors, fire extinguishers, and first aid kits. It is also essential to read reviews from previous guests to get an idea of the safety and security of the property.

Where Are Nearby Amenities?

Other common concerns travelers have when considering staying outside of a hotel for business include the location of the accommodation, the availability of amenities, and the quality of the property. To ensure a smooth and comfortable trip, it is important to research the location and surrounding area before booking. This includes checking the proximity to public transportation if this is something you desire, grocery stores for supplies, restaurants, and other essential services.

What are the In Unit Amenities included?

It is also important to check the availability of amenities like Wi-Fi, free parking, laundry facilities, cooking facilities, outdoor space, Cable TV amenities and 24-hour or other hours of check-in available.

Setting up Your Traveling Office Tips

As more professionals turn to vacation rentals and short-term apartments for business travel, it is important to find ways to stay productive and maintain a professional environment while on the go. One way to increase productivity is to use the TV in the unit as an extra monitor. Simply bring along an HDMI cord to connect your laptop to the TV, and you will have a larger display to work with. This can be particularly helpful for those who need multiple screens to work efficiently and comfortably.

Another way to boost productivity is to create a designated workspace within your accommodation. This could be a dining room table, a desk in a spare bedroom, or by moving furniture around to create an office that works for you. Having a separate workspace can help you to focus on your work and avoid distractions during your stay.

If you anticipate needing to print documents during your stay, consider stopping by an office supply store before check-in and purchasing a small printer and minimal printing supplies. This will allow you to print confidential documents without risking your privacy or security, as you would when using a public computer or hotel business center. Additionally, having a printer in your accommodation can save time and eliminate the hassle of finding a print shop while on a business trip.

The Importance of Staging Your Video Background

For those who need to participate in live meetings via video conferencing, it is important to have suitable backgrounds for Zoom or other platforms in your unit if you do not want to use a virtual background. When selecting your accommodation, consider whether the unit offers appropriate background or if you need to bring your own props. Having a professional background can help maintain a polished image during important meetings and prevent distractions from the background.

A few Cons of Using Vacation Rentals Instead of a Hotel for Business Travel

Vacation rentals and short-term apartments have become popular alternatives to hotel rooms for business travelers due to the many benefits they offer. However, it is important to be aware of the potential drawbacks that come with using this type of accommodations. Here are some cons to consider:

1. Limited on-site personnel to provide other amenities: While hotels often offer a variety of amenities such as room service, fitness centers, and on-site restaurants, vacation rentals and short-term apartments may have limited options in these categories available.

2. Inconsistent quality: The quality of vacation rentals and short-term apartments can vary widely, and there is always a risk of ending up in a property that does not meet your expectations. Although most platforms offer reviews and ratings to help travelers make informed decisions, it is important to do your research and read reviews carefully.

3. If you find yourself in unsuitable accommodations, especially if it is not as advertised, call the platform at once for assistance and resolution with the host if they are unresponsive or to be relocated if necessary.

   Unexpected things happen even in well maintained units.

   Be reasonable on workable solutions after you notify the host there is an issue just like you would in any other facility offering accommodations.

   If the hot water heater bursts while you were out putting water all over the unit, the owner will rectify this as soon as possible. They cannot fix it in 5 minutes. It is not possible.

   Hint: NEVER leave your electronics sitting on the floor!

4. Limited support: Unlike hotels, which typically have staff available 24/7 to assist guests with any issues or concerns, vacation rentals and short-term apartments may have limited support available. This can be especially problematic if you

encounter issues such as broken appliances or plumbing problems.

Be reasonable. If you reach out with an issue at 11:30 pm, the owner may not check messages until the following morning.

5. Location: Vacation rentals and short-term apartments may not always be in convenient areas for business travelers. While some may be situated near business districts or convention centers, others may be in more residential areas that require longer commutes.

6. Availability: Depending on the city or region you are visiting; vacation rentals and short-term apartments may not be as widely available as hotel rooms. This can make it more challenging to find suitable accommodations particularly during peak travel seasons.

7. Security: While vacation rentals and short-term apartments can offer more privacy than hotels, they may also have less robust security measures in place. This can make them more vulnerable to theft or other security issues. Check the listing amenities and ask about safety features before booking if this is a concern.

8. Points or frequent user rewards may not be available due to the nature of individual owners and unrelated owners.

Overall, while vacation rentals and short-term apartments offer many benefits for business travelers, it is important to weigh the pros and cons carefully before deciding. By doing your research and selecting a reputable platform or host, you can minimize the risks and enjoy a comfortable and productive business trip.

By choosing accommodations outside of the standard cookie cutter room that suit your specific needs, business travelers are discovering they can have a more comfortable and successful stay outside of a traditional hotel.

Renting a vacation rental or short-term apartment can be an excellent alternative to traditional hotel stays for business travel.

If you found value in the tips and information in this book, please reach out to schedule an appointment for individualized assistance or drop me a note to let me know what chapter was most meaningful to you.

ACKNOWLEDGMENTS

Without the support of many over the years, I could not be the person I am today. I know I will forget to thank someone, but it was not my intention to do so.

To my family, who do not always understand me, but love me anyway, you mean the world to me.

To friends and colleagues who support my professional talents and literary dreams, I wish you continued success in your endeavors.

To my talented VA team who helped me to have the finished content in print form, may your dreams come true too.

To the online writing groups from around the world on Zoom meetings where we encouraged each other in the manuscript writing processes, I did it and so can you!

To my clients and live audiences who helped me learn so much about this topic with the sharing of their life stories of successes and failures for me to give guidance to you today, thank you for allowing me to have a positive impact on your lives.

To my mentors, I promise to pay it forward.

To my draft version reviewers with all the helpful suggestions and encouragement to get this finished quickly, you will see many of your suggestions incorporated.

And finally, to all the ones behind the scenes we take for granted that make websites, online ordering, eBooks, printing, shipping, and delivery possible for us all…a heartfelt thank you for being a part of my world every day.

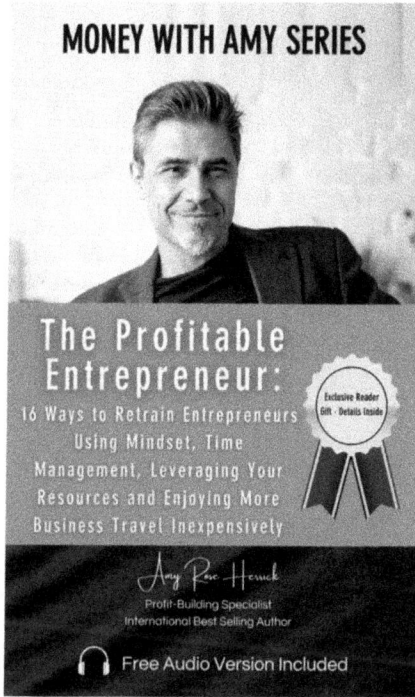

MONEY WITH AMY SERIES

The Profitable Entrepreneur:
16 Ways to Retrain Entrepreneurs Using Mindset, Time Management, Leveraging Your Resources and Enjoying More Business Travel Inexpensively

Exclusive Reader Gift - Details Inside

Amy Rose Herrick
Profit-Building Specialist
International Best Selling Author

Free Audio Version Included

THANK YOU FOR READING MY BOOK!

As a thank-you, we'd love to send you a free bonus book- not for sale anywhere else. Just email us at INFO@AmyRoseHerrick.com with "Bonus Book Request" in the subject line. You'll receive your exclusive gift directly by email.

Loved the book? We'd be grateful for your honest review on Amazon— but the bonus is yours either way.

About the Author

Amy Rose Herrick, ChFC, is an extraordinary author and financial expert dedicated to transforming lives while empowering individuals and businesses to achieve unparalleled financial success.

Some remarkable solutions take 15 minutes or less to understand and implement.

Her expertise shines brightest creating personalized, comprehensive plans that streamline costs, provide peace of mind, and secure wealth for future generations.

Bid farewell to financial stress while embracing your legacy that will endure the test of time.

Amy, your personal wealth building guide, unleashes the power within your resources.

Complex resource management problems are transformed into easy step by step solutions.

Using groundbreaking methodology, Amy empowers individuals, business owners, and families alike.

Entrepreneurs flock to Amy for clear, actionable tutorials on building more profitable businesses. Under her guidance, ventures can thrive like never before, unlocking their true potential for financial success.

As a fiduciary, Chartered Financial Consultant, and tax professional, Amy has mastered the art of optimizing resources.

Yet, her achievements do not stop there. She is a #1 Best Selling Author, captivating speaker, talented artist, and a dedicated force in community service.

With over three decades of experience, including more than 25 years in the Securities industry, Amy possesses an impressive array of qualifications and expertise. She equips you with the tools to experience lasting financial freedom, providing a transformative journey unlike any other.

In 2024, be prepared for the launch of a series of game-changing books and captivating YouTube videos titled "Money With Amy."

Her dynamic and easy-to-understand content will empower you to strategically structure your resources for the benefit of your family and businesses.

Amy Rose Herrick's list of remarkable accomplishments is truly awe-inspiring. From being named Small Business of the Year to being a #1 Best Selling Author, a National Geographic 'Chasing Genius' Finalist, and even teaching a gorilla named Max, Amy's impact is undeniable.

Clients can expect an unforgettable, life-changing experience with Amy Rose Herrick, one that simply cannot be replicated elsewhere.

Currently residing by the sea in the breathtaking US Virgin Islands, Amy continues to live a life of abundance while sharing her wealth of knowledge with the world.

For Additional Information & Resources

Visit Amy's website: **www.AmyRoseHerrick.com**

Email: **Amy@AmyRoseHerrick.com**

Book a 15-minute Zoom based discovery call to discuss becoming a client for comprehensive financial planning or business profit building assistance at:

https://calendly.com/amyroseherrick/15min

Follow Amy on Facebook

https://www.facebook.com/AmyRoseHerrickProfitBuildingSpecialist

Listen to several Podcast appearances on a variety of topics:

https://www.listennotes.com/search/?q=amy%20rose%20herrick&sort_by_date=0&scope=episode&offset=0&language=Any%20language&len_min=0

Reach out to Amy at Amy@AmyRoseHerrick.com to inquire about booking Amy to be on your show as a guest or for autographed copies.

Watch one of Amy's full length financial literacy building educational videos on YouTube

https://www.youtube.com/@amyprofitspecialist

Linked in: https://www.linkedin.com/in/amyroseherrick/

Instagram: amyroseherrick

Other titles available now, or coming soon, in the **MONEY WITH AMY SERIES** that may be of interest to you:

MONEY WITH AMY SERIES

Self-Employed Taxes:
Unleashing Schedule C Deductions A Line-By-Line Guide to Unlock Deductions and Create New Tax Savings for Small Business Owners and Independent Contractors

Exclusive Reader Gift - Details Inside

Amy Rose Herrick
Profit-Building Specialist
International Best Selling Author

Free Audio Version Included

MONEY WITH AMY SERIES

Building your
foundation:
ENTREPRENEURIAL
MISTAKES TO AVOID

Exclusive Reader
Gift - Details Inside

Amy Rose Herrick

Profit-Building Specialist
International Best Selling Author

Free Audio Version Included

MONEY WITH AMY SERIES

Protecting Your Health and Wealth:
Your Step-by-Step Guide for Multi-Generational Medical Planning

Exclusive Reader Gift - Details Inside

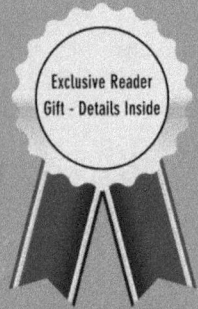

Amy Rose Herrick

Profit-Building Specialist
International Best Selling Author

🎧 Free Audio Version Included

MONEY WITH AMY SERIES

HOW TO IDENTIFY A QUALIFIED ADVISOR

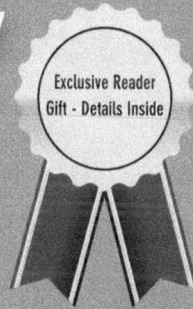

Exclusive Reader Gift - Details Inside

Amy Rose Herrick

Profit-Building Specialist
International Best Selling Author

🎧 Free Audio Version Included

MONEY WITH AMY SERIES

MARRIAGE AFTER
RETIREMENT:
25 QUESTIONS TO ASK
AND ANSWER
BEFORE YOU MARRY

Exclusive Reader
Gift - Details Inside

Amy Rose Herrick

Profit-Building Specialist
International Best Selling Author

🎧 Free Audio Version Included

MONEY WITH AMY SERIES

KNOWING YOUR LIFE PARTNER:

25 QUESTIONS TO ASK AND ANSWER (FOR COUPLES IN THEIR FIRST LONG TERM RELATIONSHIP)

Exclusive Reader Gift - Details Inside

Amy Rose Herrick

Profit-Building Specialist
International Best Selling Author

🎧 Free Audio Version Included

MONEY WITH AMY SERIES

REMARRIAGE:
25 QUESTIONS TO ASK
AND ANSWER
BEFORE REMARRIAGE

Exclusive Reader
Gift - Details Inside

Amy Rose Herrick

Profit-Building Specialist
International Best Selling Author

🎧 Free Audio Version Included